MARRIAGE MEDICINE VOLUME 5

"Love Letters"

MARRIAGE MEDICINE VOLUME 5

"Love Letters"

JESSICA SELVY-DAVIS

PO Box 1212 West Memphis, AR 72303

ISBN: 978-1-71695-128-2

DEDICATION

THIS BOOK OF LOVE LETTERS IS DEDICATED TO THE BELIEVERS OF JESUS CHRIST. PLEASE BE ASSURED THAT WE HAVE A FATHER WHO CARES ACCORDING TO HEBREWS 4:15, "FOR WE HAVE NOT AN HIGH PRIEST WHICH CANNOT BE TOUCHED WITH THE FEELING OF OUR INFIRMITIES; BUT WAS IN ALL POINTS TEMPTED LIKE AS WE ARE, YET WITHOUT."

TABLE OF CONTENTS

FOREWORD

No waiting wife left behind is all I can say. This is not only for those who are already married, but for those who hope to be married someday. One phrase that comes to mind after reading this is what's the rush?" Take your time and prepare. Take the healing salve from Marriage Medicine for it truly gives that blessed assurance to those waiting. God loves us we are not less than. He isn't punishing us. This time is necessary and only because He wants us to win. You can wait well with this preparation guide. Through this writer, hear God cheering you on. Surrounded by such a great cloud of witnesses here. You got this! We got this!

~Michelle Byrd

Whew!!! Now this was a setup and definitely needed right now. I see waiting, after I thought I had waited long enough, is very difficult. Well, for me it is. I bless God for you having the heart of God and an ear to his mouth. I had JUST asked God for instructions and here it is in a heartfelt letter. After realizing that I NEEDED to be healed AND whole, I have been just stuck on "where do I go next?" MY GOD, I have NO MORE EXCUSES for being stuck. I can progress on because of your obedience to release the heart of God towards me.

~Ms. Whitney

There are so many women who live out their lives never knowing their worth. They view themselves through the many different labels given by man. Upon reading this letter, you will be given an opportunity to see yourself through the eyes of God. Author Jessica Davis has a profound way of uncovering truth concerning our roles as wives. Her prophetic release is delivered with enough grace and simplicity to bring restoration to the confused and weary. With intimate details, she will open your eyes to your inner beauty and with inspired truth from heaven you will become the bride you were born to be.

~Mrs. Shelia Pearson

As a divorcee and a mother of two, as I read the Love Letter "Dear Divorcee," the words leaped off the page and into my heart. The letter is an awesome, amazing tool to help you confront YOU. It will make you take a good look at the person you are and ask yourself "who do I want to be?" "Do I want to be the loving person that I know that I am, but got lost in being a wife, a mother, a friend, caregiver, cook, etc. Or do I want to be bitter?" This letter is a mirror to your soul and no one has the answer, but you. It will help (make) you take a good look at yourself AND SEE WHO YOU REALLY ARE. It will teach you to take responsibility to be better and not point blame. It will also help HEAL YOUR SOUL and teach you how to truly love the person you are. About the author, for her to write such a powerful assessment on divorce and being married for over 14 years explains her depth, dedication, and RELATIONSHIP with God the FATHER. Marriage Medicine Volume Five will heal you.

~Ms. Patricia Crume

One of the most beautiful things God created in the world is covenant. Marriage is a covenant God (the groom) made on earth to show the reflection of his communion with us (the bride). From the beginning this relationship was meant to never be broken, no matter the what. Like a husband in the natural need his wife to help him get the vision God gave him completed. Likewise, God the husbandman himself need us, his wife, to help him get his Glory shown international, which is his overall vision. Despite hardship, trials and tribulations we need each other. We believe that when God joins a man and a woman together, they'll make it through anything simply knowing this, "THEY WERE BUILT FOR EACH OTHER." We've been married 7 years and God has showed us that when we hold our position down and help strengthen and encourage one another as husband and wife, we will continue to succeed. Reading the Marriage Medicine "Love Letters" has really pointed out the importance of our position in marriage as well the position we have as God's bridge. This book is definitely an antidote for husbands and wives world-wide.

~Brazell and Victoria Mathis

INTRODUCTION

Do you casually flip through the Bible, hoping a verse or passage will hit you when you need it? Or do you only read scripture as you encounter it in your daily devotional? Are you satisfied with sporadic times with God, mostly meeting Him on the run? Well as for me, I love the Bible and cling to verses that God give me when I need them however, sometimes it isn't enough. In the midst of trials while trying to figure out what to read, I began to ask God to reveal his heart to me. I had no idea how life-giving hearing him speak a rhema word would become. God's word, logos and rhema, felt like his love letter to me and changed me forever. Life can be painful and so demanding that you feel as if a single Scripture from days or months ago isn't enough to sustain you.

I encourage you to be like Jacob, who wouldn't let God go until he blessed him, beg God not to let you go until he speaks to you. Without fail, He will. Familiar passages will take on new meaning and unfamiliar ones will bring a fresh perspective. I found a joy that I had not previously experienced so consistently in the Word. Since then, scripture has felt like God's daily love letter to me. I am learning to hear God's voice and to notice what he's telling me. It's a remarkable blessing and I am praying you would find that same delight as you are reading this book of Marriage Medicine: Love Letters.

I strongly believe that sitting with God, reading His word, asking Him to share his thoughts and plans towards you, will change you. It takes discipline and practice, and growth may feel slow, but the results over time are rewarding. Each day as you read, say to God: "Speak Lord, your servant is listening". (1 Sam 3:9) I'd love to hear how He used this book of love letters to transform you.

A real love letter is made of insight, understanding, and compassion. Otherwise it's not a love letter. A true love letter can produce a transformation in the other person, and therefore in the world. But before it produces a transformation in the other person, it has to produce a transformation within us.
-Thich Nhat Hanh

CHAPTER ONE

"DEAR HUSBAND"

Let me start by saying, I love you with an everlasting love! I remember it like it was yesterday, after creating the heavens and the earth it was formless and empty as my spirit hovered over the waters in the darkness that was over the surface of the deep. After which I saw that light was good, but I saw that it needed to be separated from darkness. I called the light "day" and the darkness I called "night." There was evening and there was morning all done on the first day.

The second day I separated the water under the vault and called it sky. The third day there was land, sea, seed-bearing plants and trees. The sun, moon and stars came out of four days of creativity and I still wasn't done. For the next few days, I put in work creating the great creatures of the sea and every living thing with which the water teems and that moves about in it, according to their kinds, every winged bird according to its kind, the livestock, the creatures that move along the ground and the wild animals, each according to its kind. Yet there was still something missing, YOU! I needed mankind made in our image and in our likeness to rule over everything else I'd made. I was so pleased with my creation of you that I blessed you, instructed you and released you to dominate.

Boy I was a proud father! So much that I didn't want you to be alone, it just wasn't good. I couldn't risk you trying to convince me that you were good being alone, so I put you in a deep sleep and took your rib out and made for you a suitable helper. When you saw her for the first time you knew right away, she was yours.

It was something about her that was different from the rest and you want to know what it is? SHE IS YOUR GIFT! She's not perfect, but she is perfect for you and I need you to love her just as I loved my church. Cover her, Cultivate her, Commit to her, Continue forgiving and forsaking others for her, Compliment her, Correct her in love, Care for her, Caress her, Communicate with her, Cuddle with her, Commune with her and Create a God-like environment for her. I gave her to you so the you can love her like me in the earth. Although it's not always easy, you have within you everything it takes to be the husband I created in Genesis 1. Don't let the enemy convince you that your mistakes, failures, flaws, disappointments and doubts are enough to keep you from getting there. I love you and I am with you through it all; the good, bad and the ugly. I write this letter as a reminder that you are never defeated. You are indeed victorious as a husband. The same creativity I used to create you, use it to bring into existence what you want to see in your marriage. I am opening your heart and showing you the man that I created you to be. I know you didn't have a lot of affirming while growing up, but I want to say that you mean a lot to your family. You are worth more than you think. You are needed. I've stretched you in ways you didn't think would happen, being a husband for sure, but you have shown a lot of growth since your wedding day. Just as I became the living embodiment of a bridegroom and a faithful husband who was willing to give up my life for the ones I loved, I am gracing you to do the same according to Ephesians 5:25-27.

From My Heart,
God

CHAPTER TWO

"DEAR WIFE"

Let me start off with, YOU ARE ENOUGH MY BELOVED! How? I'm glad you asked. When I made man, he was good, but I saw that it wasn't good for him to be alone. It was at that moment I thought of you. Yes! Taking his rib to make you was the perfect idea. The look in his eyes when he saw you was priceless. Forming you from a physical part of man, was truly his complement, an integral part of who he was. As such, you are a perfect companion created to be "beside" your husband. I made man to be the provider, and I made you to be his encourager. I made man to be the protector, and I made you to be his nurturer. I made the man physically strong, but I made you soft, gentle, and tender. To be a helper to your husband on my behalf is not just an obligation, but a gift. How different your marriage would be if you rediscovered this!
I not only gave you inherent worth, I also gave you assigned worth by giving you something important to do with your life such as reproduce and partner with your husband's vision for your family. You are of great worth in my eyes and my desire is that you find great satisfaction in cooperating with my plan. You were made for man. (1 Corinthians 11:9) My crowning creation. The mother of all things. I built you to be admired by man. Not to be hit or thrown down or handled roughly or verbally beaten but to be handled delicately.

You are his glory and your desire shall be for him. No worries you have what it takes to meet his insufficiency. Again, I want you to understand that you are intellectually, morally, spiritually the gift to man. You are unique. You are smart. Your price is far above rubies. You are exceptional. Your role is like none other and although you are under the leadership, protection, and care of your husband you shine bright like a diamond. You have all the same characteristics of self-consciousness, cognition, spirituality, personality, relationship, emotion, creativity and strength. That's right, all the responsibility that I've given to him I've also given to you. I know at times it seems that your submission and service to your husband is often unnoticed and/or taken for granted. In fact, no one pays you to change your baby's diapers. No one gives you bonuses or overtime for watching sick children through the night. No one gives you certificates of appreciation for instilling moral values into your home, and there are no award banquets to recognize a job well done in the daily grind of household chores. But didn't I promise to be your very present help, never to leave you? I honor you and so very proud of the Queen I see. It takes a Queen to keep a King. Keep praying for him. Keep pushing him. Keep provoking him. Keep pleasing him. Keep pleasuring him, and I'll keep increasing your value. The Proverbs 31 woman was successful in business, but that is not what gave her value. Deborah was successful in a leadership, but that is not what gave her value. Hannah had children, one of whom was Samuel the prophet, but that is not what gave her value. Elizabeth had a great husband, Zechariah the priest, and bore John, the forerunner of Jesus, but that is not what gave her value. Mary bore Jesus, but that is not what gave her value. Your true value is centered on your faithfulness in knowing and following my will and not your own selfish desires.

Do not compare yourself to others because I am pleased with my creation of you. Rejoice in the fact that with infinite wisdom and grace that I have given you the wonderful privilege of being a woman; the help your husband couldn't do without.

From my heart,
God

CHAPTER THREE

"DEAR WAITING HUSBAND"

Every King need HIS Queen! There is nothing like having the perfect mate to travel along the journey of life. What makes it special is when you have chosen someone that not necessarily shares all the interests you have, but at least respects them and you respect hers as well.

Sure, marriage has its challenges. The key is choosing the right mate from the very beginning. By the end of this letter, I hope to have shared a bit of wisdom on how to choose a wife wisely and carefully. Physical beauty, wonderful words, affection, and sexual prowess are things that some men signal in on initially. Sometimes, these things become the predominant reasons to begin and continue a relationship. While they are important, they should not be the highest priorities in engaging in a long-term relationship that could lead to marriage. The woman you marry should have many of the same beliefs and interests as you. This doesn't mean that she can't have her own. It means that there should be interests and beliefs you have in common. It's fine to have differing opinions. But it's important that you agree on the big things – money, family, children, sex, etc. Have these discussions with the woman you're considering choosing for a wife before you marry her, to make sure you'll get along. She should be brought up in a loving home or at least have strong values and a good understanding of family life. She should respect herself and love ME! She should have good manners. If the woman you are considering marrying don't fear me, rude, uses a lot of profanity, looks down on others, is excessively moody, argumentative over minor things and/or is generally ill-tempered, DO NOT MARRY HER! This type of person will turn on you and make your life miserable. It is best she be left to her other unmarried female friends. Leave them to whine and commiserate over why no man wants to be with them in marriage. Maybe she will finally figure it out. A good wife will have achievements and successes that made her successful long before you came around. When you choose a wife, choose someone who has goals and aspirations in life that go beyond wanting to get married. Marry someone that is well educated. By this, I do not mean someone who has numerous degrees. I am talking about someone that is versatile and can have a discussion on various topics. Is she attractive to you? Again, I am not just talking about looks here. Does this woman attract you? Are you drawn to her? Is her quirky humor something you love and do her dimples make your heart melt? She doesn't have to be a celebrity housewife, but there's got to be something about a woman, more than externally, that makes you want to choose her as a wife. Does she have a sense of humor? Life is not only about work, kids, career, etc. Life and marriage should also include loads of laughter, fun and humor. DO NOT MARRY a woman who is always angry and/or depressed and doesn't laugh at the silliest things. Laughter and fun should come easy and not be forced. You should be able to laugh AT each other when appropriate and WITH each other.

Your emotional, physical and financial security depends on you knowing how she acted in previous relationships, if any. Find out as subtlety as possible. Don't interrogate her or her friends and family like the FBI! However, you can ask me to show you. If you are listening carefully, watching closely for non-verbal signs, etc., the truth will be revealed. Let her know that you are not the man she was with previously. When necessary, let this be known clearly and unequivocally. Be very clear, if necessary, that you will not be disrespected nor mistreated, in any way. Truth is, she expects the same from you. Actions speak louder than words. Some of the best liars are outstanding communicators. That's what make them great at deceiving others. It is not what she says, it's how she says it and what she does. If your car stops on a less travelled road, will she get out of bed to come and get you without debate? Does she comfort you when you are sick? Does she side with you when you are right, even at the expense of losing a good friend, who is obviously wrong? Is she supportive of your career aspirations? Does she accept you for the wonderful person you are or is she attempting to change you? Don't just listen to her "say" she loves you. Observe "how" she loves you. It is important that as a King you exemplify all of the things you want in a Queen. Learn to communicate well. Be romantic. Clear up financial problems and be up front about them. Be able to converse on topics other than sports and politics. Be truthful even if it hurts. (DO NOT MARRY a woman that can't handle the truth). Respect and take part in that for which she has a passion. Be helpful. Be respectful, don't be rude. Watch your manners. Be supportive and appreciative of all that she does for you. Do not be verbally or physically abusive (if it ever comes close to this, just walk away - forever). Do not engage her in useless arguments (be firm and resolute; she will get the message soon enough). Clearly communicate the expectations of commitment in the relationship and the ramifications if it is broken. Tell her you love her, often. Touch her affectionately and playfully. Surprise her with unexpected gifts. Dress appropriately and stay well groomed, she'll love that. With so many marriages ending in divorce, it is important for you to choose wisely and carefully in the very beginning. There are many good women that would love to have a charming, wonderful man. Keep being the best man that you can be, seeking me and asking me for guidance and you will spiritually connect to the right woman, who will ultimately be a great wife.

From My Heart,
God

CHAPTER FOUR

"DEAR WAITING WIFE"

Your Wait will not be Waisted! Know that wherever you are divorce, widowhood, long-term singleness or short-term singleness there is a journey that you must take called wholeness. First things first: you must learn how to be happy alone especially after past relationships I never authorized. Although being single is part of who you are now, it's not your final reality, I AM with you always. I love you! I want you! I adore you and preparing the best for you! Waiting takes having faith in your ability to start anew from right here, where you are today. I need you to believe that I am able to transform your present life and your very being into something more wonderful than you've ever imagined. But know that you must grant me your inner consent. I'm able, according to your faith. Be still and know that I am your God. This relationship requires balance, attention, time, and energy, just like the relationship you're seeking with Mr. Right. Put me first, and the right relationship will be added to your life when I see it's the best thing for US. I will never send you anyone to take my place. I'm a jealous God and having other Gods before me irritates me. I know you want to be found and fall in love with the right man but there are a few things I want you to be sure of before I present you to him as his suitable wife. What's going on in your heart, soul, spirit, and mind? What would I find if I searched the depths of each one? If you think you're emotionally healthy, you're wrong. If you believe you're spiritually centered and whole, you're lying to yourself. The truth is you need work! You need healing, insight, wisdom, and freedom from unhealthy soul ties. You're "in progress," and on your way to being completely healthy and whole. Mr. Right or not, you need to always be growing while simultaneously resting in My love and grace. Being aware that you need some cleaning up, means that you're on the right road. The problems come when you're deceiving yourself, or when you're believing lies about yourself. Find someone you trust to be accountable to and stay on course.

While you're waiting you should ask yourself, "do I really have time, energy, and space in my life right now for the right relationship?" It's okay if you don't because now you know what to do while you're waiting for Mr. Right. Detox your life! Figure out how to make space in your schedule for a man, and for all the demands a relationship takes. While you wait let go of and heal from the past. Truth is, if you're struggling to let go of someone you once loved, you're not ready for Mr. Right. If you're bitter or angry about a past relationship, then it's not the right time to be searching for what to do while you're waiting for a new man! If you're hung up on issues or problems from your childhood, then you need to put your quest for Mr. Right on hold for now. Find you a therapist. Heal. Find freedom and peace. Get help for your hurting heart and healing for your broken spirit. Spend time asking me to show you where you're wounded and heal your deep aches. Learn more about Me. Listen for My voice; ask me to tell you what to do while you're waiting for the right relationship. Trust me – it'll be worth it! Take time to get as emotionally and spiritually healthy as you can, and your dating life will take care of itself. Actually, I will take care of it, but you won't have to work nearly as hard as you've been doing! Knowing yourself and getting healthy will not only help prepare you to meet Mr. Right, it'll help you become Ms. Right! Instead of self-doubt, make the change to self-respect. Get it into your head that you are strong, smart, wonderful and beautiful. The King I have prepared for you will see that you are a valuable Queen. You still deserve to be treated like the respectable woman you were made to be so don't get so caught up in wanting a wedding that you forget that a marriage comes after that. It's not just a big day to celebrate with family and friends; it's a lifetime commitment to another individual.

Waiting helps you make sure that individual is actually the man you want to wake up beside for the rest of your life. I know the idea of the waiting process gets tiring but there is no set timeline for being found by the right man. A good man, the right man, is more than worth the wait. Waiting Wives, LISTEN, PLEASE do not settle for someone just because you are bored or lonely. That guy can't ever make you the happiest you were made to be, and you can't love him the right way either. If you don't wait for the person made for you, you'll end up with SOMEONE ELSE'S PERSON. That is no fun. When you're with

YOUR person, you know he's your person. You can see it in his eyes and feel it in every single embrace. It's a beautiful, moving, soul-shaking feeling. It's what you've been praying for. Do you want to settle for the so-so feeling or wait it out and get the butterflies, the really big butterflies, every single day?

Every single person in this world is different. One woman might find her Prince Charming while she's in college, and another might not meet him until after she's hit 30 or even more intimidating to some after she's had her over-the-hill party when she turned 40. Age doesn't have to be a factor for finding love. Your timeline might turn out differently than you dreamed it would be when you were a little girl watching fairytale movies or dreaming about your future. And there is nothing wrong with that, but my timing is perfect. Let me warn you, there is no perfect man, but there is someone I love who is perfect for you. So, wait for him. He's worth it. And so are you!

From My Heart,
God

CHAPTER FIVE

"DEAR DIVORCEE"

Beyond the legalities of who gets and pays what, it's important to devote time and resources to your emotional health when going through a divorce. Ask yourself these questions as you are going through the process to ensure that you will come out with your heart intact: Are you harboring any bitterness or unforgiveness toward your soon-to-be ex? Before you answer with a quick "no," it's helpful for you and for your children if you objectively evaluate your reactions and motives. If you do things like stick strictly with the custody schedule because you don't want to give him any more time with the kids, you need to check your motives. In fact, here is a checklist to make sure that your heart is in the right place:

• Do you truly wish for your kids to not like your ex or anyone that is involved with him or her?
• Do you feel pangs of jealousy when you hear about what a great time your children had with your ex?
• Do you feel as if you need to compete to make sure your ex doesn't "win"?
• Do you feel as if your ex "owes you" for all you've done for him or her or for all that he or she has done to you?
• Do you talk repeatedly about your ex and shed him or her in a bad light to others?
• Do you get angry at others who still choose to be friendly with your ex?

Only an honest evaluation will begin to reveal the condition of your heart. If you choose to move forward carrying any form of bitterness, resentment, revenge or unforgiveness, it will only be a matter of time before your life as well as your children becomes infected by it while your ex-spouse moves forward. If you are already walking through the divorce process and are praying for light at the end of the tunnel, there is hope. Many people believe (although most will never admit it) that another relationship is the answer. If they could just find someone who is or who isn't; who does or who doesn't, then all will be well. This simply isn't true. If you are not healed and whole you bring more of your brokenness into another relationship.

Emotions have a lot of energy attached to them, so the process of walking through these feelings and emotions can be a difficult and often painful experience. Creating a safe and loving environment for this process is extremely helpful and can even encourage the process to move more quickly than it might have taken otherwise. Letting go means trusting my unconditional and never-failing love in the midst of confusion and doubt.

The entire Bible is a testimony to my faithfulness and promises toward those who trust in me. No matter how the Israelites strayed from my loving care, I was constantly reaching out to them. For I, the Lord, love justice; I hate robbery and wrongdoing. In my faithfulness I will reward my people and make an everlasting covenant with them. Their descendants will be known among the nations and their offspring among the peoples. All who see them will acknowledge that they are a people the Lord has blessed. I delight greatly in the Lord; my soul rejoices in my God. *"For he has clothed me with garments of salvation and arrayed me in a robe of his righteousness, as a bridegroom adorns his head like a priest, and as a bride adorns herself with her jewels." — Isaiah 61:8-10*

Whether you experience brokenness from your own choices or through no fault of your own, you have a Savior who delights in you and desires to see you living life abundantly. As you surrender and forgive, remember that these are ongoing processes. Healing doesn't come by simply accomplishing a set of tasks, but by abiding in my love and faithfulness. Through abiding you will begin to see the fruit of your restoration. Remember, every decision regarding your thoughts, emotions and attitudes becomes a seed, and there is a daily decision to be made about whether you sow life or death into your NEXT.

From My Heart,
God

CHAPTER SIX

"WRITE A LETTER TO GOD"

Dear God,

(Share your heart)

You could be just one small adjustment away from a major win!

CHAPTER SEVEN

"DEAR READER"

In life you will have tons of things that will cause you to want to give up, a breakup, a failed career, a sickness or even a death. But throughout those things, there's God who assures, heals, provides, and encourages us to move forward every single time! Remember, God didn't promise us that life will be perfect or that it will all be candies in the sky nor it be a feeling of being in the cloud nine 24/7. Truth is, life comes with a lot of challenges that sometimes have you feeling like your life is falling apart.

Although life is uncertain God promised us that he would be there with us as we go through it all, making sure we live, we learn, and we grow. We get our hearts broken by so many things, and most times, we listen to that voice inside us that tells us to give up in life and lose hope. But here's what I learned. Whenever that voice speaks up, God also does. Listen closely. He tells us He's got this. He's got you.
He's got you when you feel broken.
He's got you when you feel frustrated.
He's got you when you feel rejected by people or even by society.
He's got you when you feel like nobody else does.
He's got you when you can't even lift yourself up.

God heals you every time you break. He picks you up every time you fall. He gives you strength when you feel weak. He fights your battles when you no longer can. And most of all, He loves you every minute of every day. He never leaves, He never forgets. He always is and always will be there. He is the love that stays, no matter the weather. So, when things get rough or feels tough, be reminded that He is GOD and he is right there to help you become a better person each day! Trust that he got you!

Sincerely,
Dr. Jessica Selvy-Davis, MP
(Mouthpiece)

MARRIAGE PRAYER

Father, we thank you again for your Word. So many thoughts flood our minds and hearts as we think about the wonder of your creation, what it was like. We thank you Lord for this, that in you we have a measure of paradise regained. We thank you, that in you we can know again the wonderful delight, joy, bliss and wonder love of marriage. That in you, marriage becomes the grace of life. That in you, we can leave and cleave in a strong bond, becoming one for life. We thank you, that in you we can enjoy communion with you as well as with each other. In you we can go, as it were, into the paradise again, and walk and talk with you in the cool of the day, as the man and the woman once could do. We thank you, that in you there is a great measure of paradise given back.

We thank you for the joys of marriage, for the blessedness of our relationship with all its richness. We thank you, Father, for showing us again the wonder of your creation and we give you all the glory. It didn't happen by chance, it didn't happen by random mutation; every single thing that came into existence, including man and woman, are made by you, by your creative hand, for your purpose. And, Father, we pray that you would cause us always to believe your Word no matter what it says, because it is, in fact, your very Word spoken to us. Father we believe that you want the best for us. You've again shown us the best is marriage: a faithful husband, faithful wife, lovingly devoted to each other for life. That's your best gift in the human realm. We thank you for it. And Lord, make our marriage what you would have it be. Fill us with grace, and fill us with the Spirit, that we may live lives that cause us to enjoy the best. Keep our marriage together; keep our marriage from sin. Keep us free from the seductions of sinful people who would seduce away my husband/wife or cause a divorce.

Restore to us the purpose and passion for our marriage so that we can enjoy each other in this life. And we know we can. We can be married for life and enjoy the sweetness and delight that you promised. And we will do it for Your glory, Thank you Jesus.

Amen.

PRAY WHILE YOU WAIT FOR YOUR MATE

Below are 15 prayers you can pray and declare daily for you and your future spouse.

1. I decree that I am fearfully and wonderfully made, and God has great plans for my life.
2. I decree my identity is not found in success, money or a mate but in being in you Jesus.
3. I decree that I will fulfill the plans of God over my life.
4. I decree I am a man or woman of purpose, honor, and integrity.
5. I declare that I am a suitable mate and will bring favor and honor to my spouse.
6. I decree that my past does not dictate my future relationships.
7. I decree that my past will not detour me but propel me deeper into God and towards the mate and life he has for me.
8. I decree that I am spiritually, physically and financially whole; I will bring something to the table.
9. I decree I will not be deceived but with clear mind, wisdom and discernment will be able to know the perfect person God has brought for me.
10. I decree that my marriage and family will prosper.
11. I decree that my mate, wherever he/she is, is being prepared to be a wonderful and suitable mate for me.
12. I pray for my future spouse's mind, and that they are rooted and grounded in you.
13. I come against any tactics of the enemy that would come to derail my future spouse and hence causing him/her to miss our connection.
14. I decree that all those around us will be blessed because of our relationship.
15. I decree that no good thing will the lord withhold from those that love him.

And it is so according to Job 22:18, *"Thou shalt also decree a thing, and it shall be established unto thee: and the light shall shine upon thy ways."* Amen

PRAYER FOR DIVORCEE

Father God, you instituted marriage as a sacred sign of love and unity between you and your bride, the Church. You gave married couples the grace they need to live together in love and harmony. Yet, that grace seems out of reach for us. Our love has ended, and our marriage has faltered. Events, which led to our separation, stir me to upset and deep regret. I come to you now in prayer, asking your mercy upon me and my former spouse that your healing may reassure both of us that your love and forgiveness remain. I ask that the problems which led to our marriage ending be an opportunity for growth in both of us, greater respect for each other, mutual pardon, deeper faith and maturity for our future spouses. Father I know that divorce is not always explainable or understandable however I ask that all involved may see our purpose in what has happened and that they and all your Church may be forgiving and understanding.

Teach me to seek after and acquire that inner submission to your will, which alone brings peace of mind. Search my heart and see that I mean my ex-spouse no ill will but wish him/her happiness now and in the future, that happiness we were unable to achieve and enjoy together with you at our center. I love you and appreciate you for your unfailing love and ask that you keep me in your care according to James 3:17, *"But the wisdom from above is first pure, then peaceable, gentle, open to reason, full of mercy and good fruits, impartial and sincere."*

Amen

APPENDIX

https://biblehub.com/kjv/hebrews/4-15.htm

https://tolovehonorandvacuum.com/2011/01/

https://tolovehonorandvacuum.com/2011/01/50-most-important-bible-verses-to/

https://www.brainyquote.com/topics/love-letters-quotes

ABOUT THE AUTHOR

Prophet Jessica Selvy-Davis is Co-Pastor and Co-Founder of Kingdom Seekers International Ministry of Arts, where she serves in ministry alongside her husband, Apostle Jonathan Davis. She is a woman who God has graced and gifted with many anointings, and she moves in them fluently and with excellence. She is an Intercessor, Mentor, Praise and Worship Leader, Author, Midwife and a Mother of many.

Prophet Jessica is fueled with a passion to advance God's Kingdom and to make His name praised in the earth. Known for her wit and sense of humor, she ministers effectively to the heart of God's people. She has a tender heart for women. She desires women to break out of the box of limitations and expand their horizon to pursue purpose and destiny. She is valued for her wisdom and intellect, and her integrity is sound. Prophet Jessica governs in the earth realm, and is determined to fulfill every prophetic word spoken over her to carry out the spiritual mandate that God has placed in her hands. She is a native of West Memphis, AR, where she serves faithfully for God's glory.

To request Prophet Jessica Selvy-Davis for speaking engagements, please email: kingdomseekers_ministryofarts@hotmail.com.

To send comments or questions please message her via
Email: lenoraselvy@yahoo.com
Facebook: https://www.facebook.com/100004940706891

Paypal- https://www.paypal.me/AuthorSelvyDavis

Cashapp- $AuthorJSDavis

www.ingramcontent.com/pod-product-compliance
Ingram Content Group UK Ltd.
Pitfield, Milton Keynes, MK11 3LW, UK
UKHW020137250726
13967UKWH00002B/706